THE  MAGIC GAMES BOOK

BARRY MURRAY

Introduction by **PAUL DANIELS**

MICHAEL O'MARA BOOKS LTD

First published in Great Britain by
Michael O'Mara Books Ltd
20 Queen Anne Street
London W1N 9FB

Text Copyright © 1989 by
Barry Murray

Illustrations Copyright © 1989 by
Michael O'Mara Books Ltd

All rights reserved. No part of this publication
may be reproduced, stored in a retrieval
system, or transmitted in any form or by any
means without the prior permission in writing
of the publisher, nor be otherwise circulated
in any form of binding or cover other than that
in which it is published and without a similar
condition including this condition being
imposed on the subsequent purchaser.

A CIP catalogue record for this book is
available from the British Library

ISBN 1-85479-000-5 (hardcover)
ISBN 0-948397-83-7 (paperback)

Cover and illustrations: The Character
Licensing Company Ltd,
Laurence Vant

Editor: Antonia Owen
Design: David Warner

Filmset by Florencetype Ltd, Kewstoke, Avon
Printed and bound in Portugal by
Printer Portuguesa

For Sam and Frankie,
My Fun and Games

INTRODUCTION

'To play, to play, perchance to win.' My apologies to William Shakespeare for paraphrasing one of his most famous lines. Sorry, Bard.

'Winning is not the important thing, it's playing the game that counts,' said Lord Baden-Powell. I'm in a name-dropping mood in this introduction. 'And why not?' as Barry Norman would say. Whoops! I did it again. Well, I can if I want to. It's my introduction to this marvellous collection of magic games.

Wizbit has found and invented some super magic games for you, for all occasions. Rainy, hazy days, sunny, lazy days – any day is a good day to open this book and pick a game to play. The props you need are everyday items that you will already have around you at home.

Actually, it's not so much playing or winning the game that matters, it's enjoying the game as you play it with your friends that really counts. Remember that.

PS Magic is a wonderfully interesting pastime. Why don't you send a stamped, self-addressed envelope to the following address?

The Wizbit Magic Club
Department 7
60 Kings Road
London SW3 4UP

You will receive, by return of post, full details on how to further your interest in all things magical.

Have fun. I know you will.

Paul Daniels

Telepathy Game

Try this really baffling card trick to amaze a group of your friends.

THE TRICK

While a friend (whom we will call the telepathic medium) is out of the room, spread about fifteen playing cards face up on the floor. Now ask somebody to select one of the cards by pointing to it.

Tell him to call the medium back into the room and then, without saying a word to her, you simply point to different cards in turn. The medium says nothing until you point to the selected card, when she suddenly calls out, 'Stop – that's the card.' And it is! The trick can be repeated two or three times.

HOW IT'S DONE

Before you even perform the trick you must choose a friend who will act as the telepathic medium, and teach her this secret code: 6 – 4 – 7 – 9.

When a card has been selected and the medium has returned to the room, begin pointing to various cards, one at a time. All she has to do is silently to count as you point. The sixth card you point to will be the selected card. To repeat the trick, the selected card will be the fourth card you point to. If you do it a third time it will be the seventh card. Only do it a fourth time if you're sure they are really baffled. Three times is usually enough.

Chuckletime

This is a fun party game for any number of players. What happens is that everybody sits down, quite still, except for one person. He is called 'the starter'. Everybody's objective is to keep a straight face, without smiling or laughing, for as long as possible.

The starter can tell jokes, tap dance, pull faces, juggle, fall over, do silly walks, anything to make his friends smile or laugh. As soon as somebody does smile or laugh, then they stand up and join the starter in attempting to make the others smile or laugh.

By the time there are only two players left with straight faces – and everybody else is trying to make them laugh – it's a riot. The winner is the one who is last to smile or laugh.

Wooly: Which way in?
Wizbit: Which way out?

Wooly: It's a duck.
Wizbit: No, it's a rabbit if you give the book a quarter turn to the right.

Impossible Balance

This party trick will amaze you and all your friends when they try it.

THE TRICK

Cut a piece of paper to the size of a five-pound note. Your mother or father will lend you one to measure, I'm sure. Fold it in half lengthways, making a good sharp

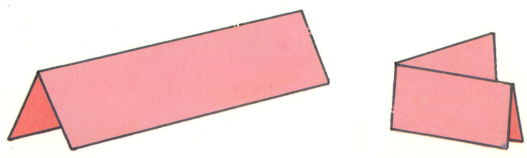

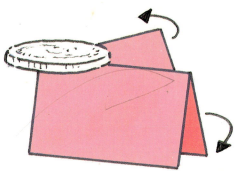

out. Curiously enough, the coin doesn't fall off. Instead it gradually changes its position to remain balanced on the creased edge of the paper, even when the paper is fully straightened out. And that's the amazing part. Because you would never be able to balance a coin on a creased paper without knowing the trick method.

crease, then fold it in half across the middle, so it looks like a letter V.

Stand it on the table with the crease upwards and balance a coin on the point of the V. That's the easy part. Now for the magic part. Grip each end of the V with your finger and thumb and very carefully, very gently straighten the piece of paper

---

Wooly: How do I eat a carrot with this?
Wizbit: Cover the points of the fork with your finger and move it up and down.
(Now you see why he's puzzled.)

Get Out Of That!

Here's another magic trick that you can try on your friends. Fill two paper cups with water. Ask a friend to hold out both hands, palms upwards. Carefully balance a cup on the palm of each hand. Then step back and say, 'Get out of that without spilling a drop of water.'

She probably won't realise how to very quickly. The quick, trick way is carefully to lift your right hand towards your mouth and bend your head forward. You will be able to drink the water, then grip the cup with your teeth. Take your right hand away and take the cup from your mouth. You are now free to drink the water in the left-hand cup.

Wizbit: Hold this at eye level and rotate quickly in small circles. See how the cog turns the wheels.

How To Put Your Head Through A Playing Card

Magicians are funny people. Why would anyone want to put their head through a playing card? Because nobody believes you can do it, that's why. And not only can you do it, your friends can as well. Here's how this magic game is played. Ask your mother or father for an old pack of cards that they don't use any more.

Fold the long sides of a playing card together and firmly crease. Then, with a pair of scissors, very carefully make eight cuts equally spaced along the length of the folded edge of the card. Don't cut right to the edges of the card. Stop a little way from the edges. Turn the card round and make seven similar cuts along the open side, in between the first set of cuts, stopping short of the folded edge. Open the card out and carefully cut along the crease from X to Y. You are ready to open the card by gently stretching it out, until you can put your head through it.

Get your friends to try it and see who has made the biggest circle. If you find the card difficult to cut, ask your mother or father to cut it for you, or you can use a postcard instead.

The secret of the trick is that the more cuts you make, the bigger the circle. You will be able to get more than your head through a postcard, maybe even your whole body. Try it and see.

I Spy Wizbit

Make a tracing of Wizbit from the accompanying illustrations, then transfer it to a piece of thin card. Colour it in and carefully cut it out with scissors – be careful, scissors are sharp. Put glue on to the flap marked *glue* and fold the cone into shape, sticking the glued flap inside the cone. Hold it in place until the glue has set. Then you are ready to play.

Tell a friend to wait outside the room while you place Wizbit somewhere in the room. He must be at least partly visible. When you are ready, call your friend in to find Wizbit. Give him no clues at all. If you want to time him you can. When he finds Wizbit it is then your turn to go out of the room while your friend hides him for you to find. Sometimes the most obvious places are the last to be noticed.

Drop Shot

Stand a Wizbit cone on the floor and sit down about 2.4 m (8 ft) from it. Your friend sits opposite you on the other side of Wizbit. Hold a balloon and knock it high into the air in such a way that it will drop on to Wizbit's point. You take it in turns and the first to get ten drop shots on target is the winner.

Wizbit: If you would like to see Wooly eat this carrot, hold the picture at eye level and slowly bring it towards your nose. Keep your eyes fixed on the spot midway between Wooly and the carrot.

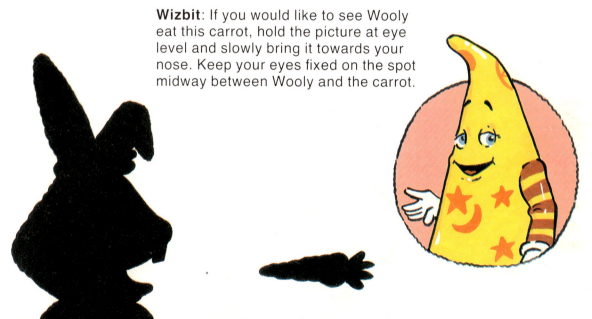

Wooly: I can't read this, Wizbit.
Wizbit: Yes you can. Just look along the page like this from bottom to top.

Personal Magnetism

Try this amusing game with your friends. Each player has to press a penny against the centre of his forehead, then take his hand away. The one whose coin stays in place the longest is the winner. You will win every time. Here's how.

Press a penny, tail side towards you, against your forehead, just above the line of your eyebrows. Then push it up about an inch to the centre of your forehead. This creates a suction, which is your secret!

Wizball

For this breathtaking game you will need one Wizbit cone, two empty matchboxes and two 21 cm (8 in) paper tubes, which you make by rolling two sheets of A4 size paper from the bottom edge into a tube and securing with Sellotape or two rubber bands, one at each end. This is your blow-tube.

The matchboxes are placed upright at each end of the table, opposite each other. Having first removed the tablecloth, lay your Wizbit cone in the centre of the table.

The object of the game is to score a goal by blowing Wizbit on to your opponent's matchbox with your blow-tube. Meanwhile he is trying to score a goal by blowing Wizbit on to your matchbox. Each game is ten minutes long and, like real football, the winner is the player who scores the most goals.

Blowing in a cone in the direction you want is not easy. There is a knack to it which you will discover the more you play the game.

Magic Memory

Did you know that memory is the thing you forget with? I'll prove it to you. With a friend, study the twenty-five objects illustrated on this page for three minutes. Use an egg-timer if possible. Then close the book and on separate pieces of paper write down as many objects as you can remember. Do not peek at your opponent's list. The person who remembers the most objects is the winner.

If you play the game by yourself, this guide will tell you how well you've done: **10** is OK, **15** is good, **20** is very good, **24** is excellent, **25** is magic.

En Garde – The Safe Sword Fight

This is a game for two energetic people. You play a safe sword fight while blindfolded. You will need two rolled-up comics or newspapers. Move the furniture in your room, if necessary, to make a clear space. Put on your blindfolds, adopt the sword-fighting stance holding your comic sword, and you're ready to play. Your opponent starts the game by saying 'En garde.' The sound of his voice will tell you where he is and you must try to hit him by striking down with your comic – not poking or prodding. Of course as soon as he says 'En garde' he moves. And then you say 'En garde' and move to one side while he attempts to hit you. And so the game goes, speaking and moving, side to side, forwards and backwards, like two expert duellists. You may even drop to the ground to avoid being hit. Of course you will bump into each other but that's half the fun. Remember you are not taking it in turns – it's a real sword fight!

The winner is the one to strike ten blows first, which may take longer to happen than you think.

Solo Pairs

This is a fascinating game for one player. Shuffle the cards and deal three rows of three cards face up on the table. The object of the game is to remove from the nine cards two cards of the same value and colour, for example two red threes. Deal more cards into the spaces left by the removed cards. Then deal nine further cards on top of the nine cards on the table.

The only rule is that no pair may be made from the same column. A pair can only be made by two cards from separate columns.

If you manage to pair off the entire pack, that will be a major achievement. If not, shuffle the cards and start again, but keep a record of the number of pairs you made in each game to see how close you get to pairing the whole pack.

STARTING LAYOUT

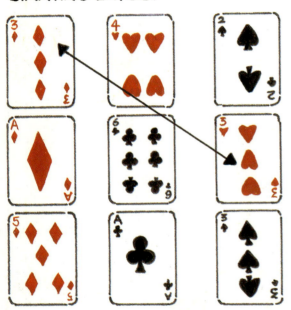

THE GAME CONTINUES

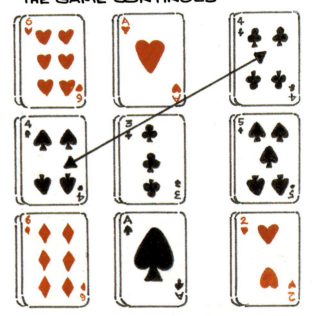

Three Stand-Up Games

The object of this game is for the contestants to walk from one end of the room to the other, touch the wall and walk back to their starting positions. It's not quite as easy as it sounds, because everybody has to do it with a folded newspaper or comic balanced on their head. Naturally some will do it quicker than others. The one who does it quickest without the paper dropping off their head is the winner.

If that seems too easy, try it with a book on your head. Then it becomes a slightly slower game. And if you want to make it slower still, put an apple on top of the book on top of your head.

I wonder if the same person will be the winner of all three games.

Wizbit: Waves are up, troughs are down, until you turn the book around.
Wooly: I feel seasick.

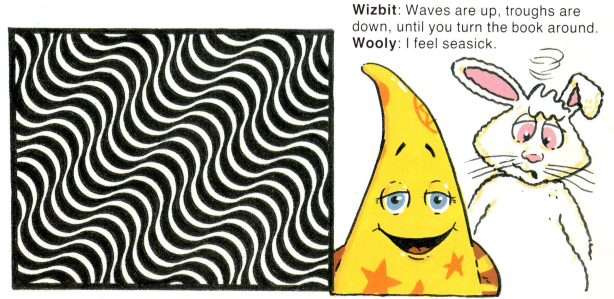

Wizshot 1

For this super target game you will need a pile of rubber bands and a balloon. The first thing I'll teach you is how to shoot a rubber band. Make a gun shape with your right hand – your forefinger stuck out like a gun barrel and thumb raised like the gun's hammer. Place the inside of a rubber band over the tip of your forefinger and stretch it around the outside of the knuckle at the base of your thumb and down, looping the other end of the band over the tip of your little finger. This will keep the band stretched. Now point at a target and pull your little finger in towards your palm, releasing the rubber band, which will shoot from your finger at great speed. With a little practice you will soon get the hang of it. One word of caution: don't shoot at any of your friends. It could

A good variation of this game is to prop a paper bag open on the floor so that it is facing you. You and your friend sit 1.8 to 2.4 m (6 to 8 ft) away on the floor. The objective is to see who can shoot the most rubber bands into the bag. If you each use different colour bands it will be easy to check who is the winner.

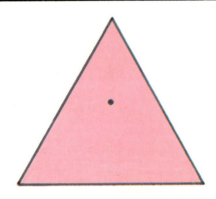

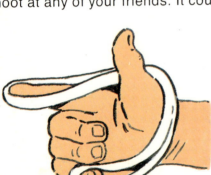

Wizbit: Is the dot exactly half-way between the base and the point of the triangle?
Wooly: No, it's too high up.
Wizbit: Measure it and see!

hurt them if it catches them in the eye and that wouldn't be funny at all.

To play the game with a friend, knock the balloon into the air and take turns shooting at it with rubber bands. The person to get the most direct hits on the balloon is the winner. For a hit to count the balloon must be in the air.

Wooly: There are four planks of wood.

Wizbit: No, there are three.

Jelly

Sit next to a friend at the kitchen table. You each have a bowl of jelly and a spoon. The object of the game is to finish eating your jelly before your friend.

Oh, there is just one thing I forgot to mention. The spoons are tied together with a piece of string, about 45 cm (18 in) long. Have fun!

Mad Shoes

Here is a terrific party game. All the boys take off their shoes and leave the room. The girls gather up the shoes and mix them up in a pile in the centre of the room. On the words 'Mad shoes!' the boys rush in and try to find their shoes. The first person to find them and put them on is the winner!

You can then play the game once more, this time putting all the girls' shoes in the middle of the room.

Wizbit's Balloony Race

Have you ever heard of an egg and spoon race? Contestants have to run, holding a tablespoon with an egg in its bowl. The first to pass the winning post without dropping and breaking the egg is the winner. It's great fun but can be very messy. So Wizbit came up with a balloon and spoon race, which is a very different thing indeed. You can race the length of a room or from one room to another and back again.

Balance your balloons in the bowls of your spoons and, when everybody is ready, shout 'Go!' You'll enjoy this game, although it's not quite as easy as it sounds. Try it and see.

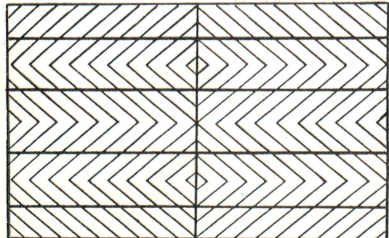

Wooly: I don't think these horizontal lines are straight, Wizbit.

Wizbit: It's amazing, but they are.

The Origami Banger Game

Take a piece of A4 paper and fold it in the following way, making each crease nice and sharp by using the edge of a ruler or pencil.

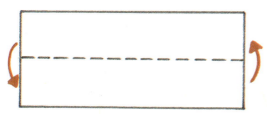

1. Long edge to long edge, crease and unfold.

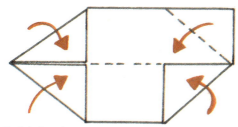

2. Fold the four corners in so they meet, crease and leave folded.

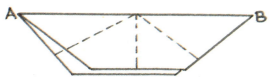

3. Refold long edge to long edge, crease again and leave folded.

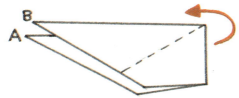

4. Fold in half so points A and B meet, crease and leave folded.

5. Fold points A and B back so they meet, crease firmly and leave folded. Now using the flat side of your ruler,

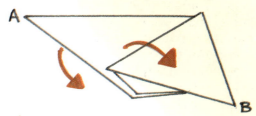

press down firmly along all the edges of the banger. Grip the banger at points A and B mouth down between your thumb and fingers and thrust downwards with a brisk-throwing action.

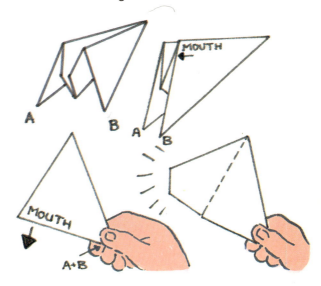

To play the banger game, make two bangers. Then unfold them and give one to a friend. The object of the game is to shout 'Go!', then to fold and shoot the banger before your opponent shoots you. Whoever folds and shoots the banger first is the winner.

Paddles

Wooly: My paddle is bigger than yours.

Wizbit: So it appears. But if the reader traces both paddles, and draws them on to a piece of thin card and carefully cuts them out, then places my paddle under yours, you'll be in for a surprise.

Tumbling Magic

Here is a marvellous magic game which is a real swindle to play on your friends.

THE TRICK

Three empty tumbers are in a row on the table in the following positions. One is mouth down, the second is mouth up and the third is mouth down. Three moves later they are all mouth up, which is the right way up. So far so good. Reset the glasses to start and invite a friend to turn the glasses mouth up in three moves as you did. Three moves later the glasses are still mixed up. You can do it. He can't.

HOW IT'S DONE

Mentally number the glasses one, two and three from left to right. One is mouth down. Two is mouth up. Three is mouth down. This is your starting position to turn the tumblers over in the following way:

Start position

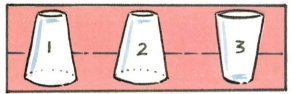
First move: turn tumblers two and three

Second move: turn tumblers one and three

Third move: turn tumblers two and three

So, to start, the code to remember is: down, up, down; then two and three, one and three, two and three.

This will leave all three glasses mouth up.

Now here is the swindle. Turn the centre tumbler mouth down and invite a friend to do as you did in three moves. It can't be done. His starting position is different to yours, but nobody will notice. So don't repeat the trick or he may spot the swindle.

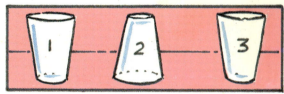
Friend's start position

First move: turn tumblers two and three

Second move: turn tumblers one and three

Third move: turn tumblers two and three

Glasses are now all mouth down instead of mouth up.

Here are Wizbit and Wooly in the Puzzlecar. If you want Wooly to drive, hold the picture at eye level and quickly rotate it in small anti-clockwise circles. If you want Wizbit to drive, rotate in clockwise circles. I wonder if they'll ever get to where they're going?

Wizbit's Magic Propellers

Here is a really good magic stunt that all your friends can try.

THE TRICK

If you ask your parents nicely they will probably get you a packet of cigarette papers from a newsagent. They are perfect for this trick. Alternatively you can cut up a number of pieces of tissue paper to the size of cigarette papers.

Take a piece of paper and carefully fold all four sides up at right-angles about 5 mm (¼ in). Then pinch each corner with your thumb and finger. This makes the paper look like a shallow tray. If you do use a cigarette paper, remember to flatten it out to take the crease out of it.

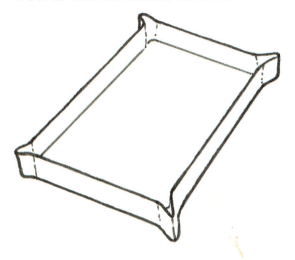

Place the centre of the underside of the tray carefully on your right first fingertip. Hold it in place with your right thumb on the topside of the tray. The position is exactly the same as putting the fingertips of both forefingers together, except you have a small paper tray held between them.

Extend your arms in front of you and start to turn round on the spot from right to left. As the air pressure begins to meet the paper tray, quickly take your thumb away and turn a little quicker. Keep turning and you will find the little paper tray spinning round just like an aeroplane propeller.

Get all your friends to do it at the same time. It looks great. But do make sure they keep their feet on the ground!

Magic Message

Get your friends to each draw a 10 cm (4 in) square, using a ruler and pen. Draw three lines down, equally spaced, and three lines across, equally spaced. This will give them sixteen squares, which is the starting point for this magic game.

Tell them to write the letters in each square as shown. Have them cut carefully with scissors along the line from A to B and place the right-hand piece on top of the left. Then get them to cut from C to D and put the top pieces on top of the bottom pieces. Then cut from E to F and place right-hand pieces on left-hand pieces. Carefully cut from G to H and put top pieces on top of the bottom pieces.

You will now have a little packet of paper squares. Deal the pieces, from the top, in a row from left to right on the table. As if by magic a message will appear.

HOW IT'S DONE

Here is a diagram that shows you the sequence in numbers, which will enable you to make your own messages. Write any message that is sixteen letters or less.

Where you want a space put in a little star. Write the first letter of your message on square 1, the second letter on square 2, and so on. Here are some suggestions:
A * HAPPY * NEW * YEAR. * HAPPY * BIRTHDAY! * I'M * A * MAGICIAN *

You can even write your friend's names and let them cut them up and lay them out. Here's a good example:
S * A * M * A * N * T * H * A!
They will be surprised!

6	2	5	1
14	10	13	9
8	4	7	3
16	12	15	11

Wooly: This looks very confuddling.

Wizbit: That's because it's an impossibleossity, Wooly!

Wizshot 2

Get hold of some straws that have paper covers and a paper bag. Open the bag and put it on the floor so that it sits with its opening towards the ceiling. Both players sit on the floor opposite each other with the bag in between them. Each should be about 1.5 m (5 ft) from the bag. The object of the game is to see who can blow the most straw paper covers into the bag. The first one to five wins.

To blow the paper covers, first tear off one end and pull the cover about 2.5 cm (1 in) down the straw. Now hold the straw, close to the end, put it to your lips, take aim and blow.

A Different Hide-and-Seek

This is a really good variation on the classic game of hide-and-seek, which everybody knows how to play. This quiet version is best for more than two players. One player goes and hides. After counting to thirty, the others go to look for him. The first of the seekers to find him quietly hides with him, as does the next seeker, and so on, until there is only one seeker left and he becomes the hider in the next game. Obviously the more places to hide, the better the game will be.

Memory Game

With a pen draw two rectangular frames onto two pieces of paper. Give one piece of paper and a pen to your opponent. Now both study the illustrations in the two frames on this page for three minutes, then close the book and put it aside. The object of the game is to reproduce the drawings from memory. The winner is the contestant – or artist – whose drawings are the most accurate.

Remember, Remember

This is a great card game for any number of players to play. Shuffle the cards thoroughly and spread them out face down over the entire surface of a table top.

The first player to go turns any two cards face up. If they are two of a kind, for example, two black sixes or two red sevens (any pair of the same colour), she removes them from the spread and puts them face down in front of her. As she made a pair, she gets another go and can turn over another two cards. If they are not a pair, she turns them face down in the position they were in. It is now the next player's turn. The winner of the game is the player who has collected the most pairs.

The key to winning the game is to remember which cards were turned up and turned down and the positions they occupied on the table.

Answers to the 'W' Game on page 19

1 Wizbit
2 Wooly
3 Wagon
4 Walking stick
5 Wall
6 Walnuts
7 Wallet
8 Wand
9 Washbasin
10 Wastepaper basket
11 Water
12 Water pistol
13 Wedge
14 Wheel
15 Whip
16 Willow-pattern plate
17 Windmill
18 Wine
19 Witch
20 Wolf
21 Wood
22 Wool
23 Word
24 World
25 Window
26 Worm
27 Writing
28 Wren